"Darbuni has long had a heart for souls, which prompted her to work with the 700 Club for over 20 years to help spread the gospel of salvation throughout Nigeria. Her ordeals have undoubtedly fueled her desire for the lost. It is no surprise that she explains concisely that "it is God's will for us all to be saved." She recognizes, however, that unforgiveness has become extra baggage that serves no one.

This book is required reading for everyone who carries the baggage of unforgiveness that is impeding their access to the good health (body, soul, and spirit) that God desires for us when He says, *"I pray that you may prosper in all things and be in health, just as your soul prospers"* (3 John 1:2, NKJV)."

—Dr. Felix Oisamoje
Regional Director,
Christian Broadcasting Network, Africa
Abuja, Nigeria

"This book is a personal story of courage and determination during difficult circumstances, emphasising the power of the unwavering human spirit and God's grace.

Darbuni's inspiring journey motivates readers to turn to God for strength in overcoming obstacles and discovering their purpose. Her sincere message provides valuable advice for navigating life's challenges and trusting in God's healing grace. I'm honoured and proud to have the author as my biological sister."

—Reverend Dunka Joseph Gomwalk
Senior Pastor,
Covenant Word Christian Centre International (CWCCI)
Chairman,
Pentecostal Fellowship of Nigeria (PFN)
Plateau State Chapter
Jos, Nigeria

"Darbuni has gifted us with a deeply moving, impactful, and potentially life-altering read. This isn't just a book. It's an EXPERIENCE. Darbuni shares her personal testimony with such sincerity and authenticity, lovingly drawing you into a time of self and life re-evaluation. Go in with an open and expectant heart. I promise you will find the Triune God ready to perform the four "Rs" in your life. Just like he has done for Darbuni."

—SALT Essien-Nelson
Chief Errand Girl,
The Sholly Smile Factory
Lagos, Nigeria

R4

R4

How To Live In Gods Healing Grace

RESET.RESTORE.RENEW.REST

Darbuni Hyai Maikori

Photography: TY Bello | IG @tybello

Illustration Design: XXIV PRO Consulting | IG @xxivpro

Book Cover Design: Raymond van der Mescht

ISBN Paperback: 978-1-961557-88-8

ISBN Ebook: 978-1-961557-89-5

Library of Congress Control Number: 2023917871

Messenger Books
30 N. Gould Ste. R
Sheridan, WY 82801

Dedication

For my two beautiful children:
May your journeys in life lead and keep you on the path
of our Lord and Saviour, Jesus Christ.
Love always, Mom

Contents

Introduction
My Daughter...the Author

When I married, I prayed to have six children, just like my mother. God was merciful and granted me my heart's desire. I gave birth to six children, and Darbuni is my youngest. She is a miracle child. This statement may sound odd, and it is only possible to explain by reflecting on past and significant events throughout her life.

Her birth was difficult and complicated. She was born blue because of severe asphyxiation and had a broken clavicle, but God miraculously revived her and healed her bones with no complications. Do you see why I call her a miracle? From the beginning, there was no mistaking that God had a purpose for her life.

Darbuni means "You Wait and See." Her father gave her this name not long before he passed on. His faith in God was so strong that he knew, despite the perilous circumstances at the time, in due course, people would see the hand of God on his family. It's been 47 years since then, and it's clear that God inspired him to name her as a loving, reassuring message of consolation and encouragement to us. My children and I have come to understand what his poser, "You Wait and See," means as we experience God's lavish love, favour, and mercies year after year. God has shown off His power in our lives. So, no matter the trials, His response to us is *"You Wait and See*; I shall work it all out for good."

She grew up in a typical Christian home, attending elementary and secondary schools as any average child, and then pursued a higher degree in the university. Immediately after concluding the mandatory Nigerian youth service with the National Youth Service Corps (NYSC), she was granted formal employment. Soon after, she married, began a family, and birthed two beautiful children.

During her second pregnancy, she became very ill. Her diagnosis was devastating and unexpected, but we immediately prayed to God and fasted. For 15 years, she suffered several courses of medical treatments and surgeries. Despite these trials, Darbuni's outlook encouraged us all. She remained courageous and active. Seemingly unconcerned about what she was going through, she persevered and raised her family. Whenever we saw or spoke to her, we couldn't tell she was dealing with such a grievous ailment.

Through it all, she excelled professionally and even returned to school to pursue a master's degree and various certifications! In the advent of the 2020 COVID-19 pandemic, she survived life-threatening surgery, medical complications, frontline exposure to the coronavirus, and severe treatments! Whatever the devil brought her way did not deter her progress in life; that can only be God. There are no explanations for how God has brought her this far or why she's still alive. I believe in my spirit that God recruited Darbuni for Himself. There's an indelible purpose in her, and the level of challenges and records of undefeated victories match God's unique calling on her life.

This book is part of the fruit of that calling. As I've watched her grow into the woman she is today, one thing is obvious: Darbuni's trust and dependence on God are critical factors in her victory story. I know my daughter; she is a very private individual. For her to put this book into your hands can only be by divine instruction. I pray that this book's purpose will be fully accomplished in the name of Jesus Christ. Amen.

I thank God for the gift of Darbuni to our family. I thank God for the courage He has given her and for sustaining her through the years. According to God's Word, I am confident that God has healed her and made her whole to fulfill what He has purposed for her to accomplish on earth.

"Ubangiji"–Almighty God, Lord.[1] "Gagara Misali"— unquantifiable God, impossible for example, or to compare. Thank you for being so faithful, merciful, gracious, loving, kind, and patient. You alone are God.[2]

I joyfully sing this Hausa song, "Ina karfin shaidan in da Yesu yana mulki? Ba bu o sam sam."[3] Translated in English, it means, "Where is the power of satan where Jesus reigns? None/Nowhere at all."

To the person reading this now, know that this God is indeed God. If you have yet to accept Jesus Christ as your Lord and Saviour, think again. Consider that life tomorrow is not guaranteed, and there won't be another chance after this life is gone. May the peace of God remain with you and lead you daily as you walk within the bounds of Jesus Christ, our Saviour. Amen.

—Mrs. Hannatu Joseph Dechi Gomwalk
Ex-Board Chairman & Member, Christian Institute,
Plateau State, Nigeria
Ex-Commissioner & Founder Girls' Brigade Band, Plateau
State Council, The Girls' Brigade Nigeria
Diocesan Merit Awardee for Christian Legacy,
Anglican Diocese of Jos, Nigeria
Merit Awardee, Women Wing Christian
Association of Nigeria
Distinguished Chorister Awardee, St. Piran's
Anglican Church, Plateau State, Nigeria

Foreword

The day we are born and the day we die are the most important days in our life, the one initiating us into this world and the other leading us into the next. Any anxiety over the day of our birth belongs to the mother and not to the child, but the day of our death is different. That day may come suddenly and unexpectedly, or some form of sickness or physical disability may give us a shorter or longer time to prepare. Having just recovered twice from stage four cancer of the colon and liver, I can identify closely with the situation in which Darbuni Dorcas Maikori found herself.

This book is a brave, open, and honest account of how a young woman faced what she thought was imminent death, with all the physical and mental pain, frustration, fear, and anxiety involved. She had been a Christian for many years, but her situation as a cancer patient required a new kind of relationship with God, with faith and trust, as she had not had earlier in her life. God gave her four keywords, which acted as a frame, support, and guide for the very tough and difficult times that she had to face: Reset, Restore, Renew, Rest. To walk in the path thus set out before her, and to stick to it, required courage, commitment, dedication, and an ever-growing faith–together with the unfailing support and encouragement of her family. She has emerged stronger in both faith and character.

This book is a remarkable testimony, written honestly and simply, relying on God at every step. It is a book which can encourage and bring hope to all Christians.

—Dr. Benjamin A. Kwashi
Bishop of Jos
Anglican Diocese of Jos,
Plateau State, Nigeria

Preface

*"Cancer is something evil or malignant
that spreads destructively."*

*"God heals us all from all sicknesses and
diseases, from the cancers of life that
fester in our spirit, body, and mind,
often unconsciously."*

Dear Reader,

My name is Darbuni Dorcas, and I am a cancer survivor. Every day I breathe is a testament to God's Healing Grace, and I give Him all the glory for repeatedly snatching me from the jaws of death throughout my life. This book is written in obedience to God and with the guidance of the Holy Spirit. In it, I share my healing journey, as well as God-given tools and resources, for victoriously surviving and thriving at every stage.

Looking back over the last 20 years, it is simply amazing how God brought me through the most perilous times of my life and, at the same time, clothed me in the beauty of my most significant blessings, victories, and achievements, the best of which was His gift of **Grace** and **Rest**.

Cancer[1] is something evil or malignant that spreads destructively. It has negative physical, spiritual, mental, and emotional manifestations that cause sickness, disease, depression, loneliness, and despondency leading to premature death. We are all exposed to various levels of cancers, individually or vicariously, and this book is for anyone dealing with, recovering from, or surviving the battle of life's cancers. There is so much going on underneath the surface of our lives, and if not adequately addressed, the cancers of life can breed and, sometimes, take hold. But glory to God! Like me, you, too, can find your path to **Reset**, **Restoration**, and **Renewal**, leading to a place of total **Rest** in God, the Healer, through Jesus Christ, our Lord and Savior.

God heals us all from all sicknesses and diseases, from the cancers of life that fester in our spirit, body, and mind, often unconsciously. I pray that, as you read this book, you experience an encounter with God and reap the harvest of God's abundant Grace and Rest. No matter what you are dealing with, if you put all your hope in Jesus Christ, you will never be alone. He will see you through all of life's difficulties. I hope you will discover, as I have, that in Christ, you can still live a fulfilling life and thrive, despite adverse circumstances. Only God has the *final* say. Enjoy the read.

Darbuni

85 PRESCRIPTION INJECTABLES
TEARS
80 BLOOD DRAWS
14 MAMMOGRAMS
FEAR
5 MAJORSURGERIES
230 SUTURES
10 PEDICAL SCREWS
2 MRIS
230 SUTURES
COUNTLESS MISTAKES
PAIN
SCARS
FEAR
50 IMPLANTS
HEARTBREAKS
PAIN
FEAR
2 MRIS
TEARS
50 IMPLANTS
14 MAMMOGRAMS
12 SPINAL TITANIUM RODS
SURGICAL STAPLES
COUNTLESS MISTAKES
SCARS
PAIN
FEAR
46 SURGICAL STAPLES
4 IMPACTED VERTEBRAE
80 BLOOD DRAWS
50 IMPLANTS
85 PRESCRIPTION INJECTABLES
FEAR
TEARS
4 BONE SCANS
5 MAJORSURGERIES
30 RADIOTHERAPY SESSIONS
12 PET-CT SCANS
10 PEDICAL SCREWS
HEARTBREAKS
3 BROKEN TOES
BETRAYAL
14 MAMMOGRAMS
3 BROKEN TOES
TEARS
FEAR
MAJORSURGERIES
BONELESIONS!
4 BONE SCANS
LUMBAR PUNCTURE
12 PET-CT SCANS
BETRAYAL
4 BONE SCANS
LUMBAR PUNCTURE
BETRAYAL
BETRAYAL
2 MRIS
COUNTLESS MISTAKES

Prologue

"Revelation: an act of revealing or communicating divine truth."[1]

The Revelation

In July 2020, my world stood still. Cancer[2] had returned; it snuck up on me and, this time, brought complications in my spine that were, not only threatening to steal my ability to walk, but also to take my life in the process. My diagnosis was terminal, the prognosis was bleak, and several vertebrae points had been impacted. I had to undergo spinal surgery fast! I prayed, cried, and reflected on my life with thanksgiving for the beautiful years God had already given me. Then, without denial, I realised that this would be it; my final days had come, or so I thought.

Life had lost its appeal; nothing mattered except the deep nagging despair of leaving my young children and considering their life without a mother to nurture, guide, and protect them as fiercely as my mother did me. Waves of fear swept over me as I contemplated the experience of death and its impact on my children.

The advent of the killer coronavirus pandemic came with so many unknown factors, travel and movement restrictions, and rising death tolls globally. Avoiding the hospital was the order of the day, yet I was scheduled for life-saving surgery in a hospital during the pandemic. Except for the mercy of God, coming out alive was something I didn't expect.

Resigned to my fate, I went before God in repentance, asking Him to search my heart, cleanse, and forgive me of all my sin.

Then, unexpectantly, a revelation came to me as I slept one evening. At that moment, I became fully aware of God's complete redemption and forgiveness of my sins. I knew God had set me free from all encumberments, and I felt a deep inner peace.

I woke up ready to take on the life-threatening surgery, knowing that no matter the outcome, it was all well. Before surgery, I arranged for memorial photos to be taken for my children, finalised my affairs, and made ready to meet God, my Maker. But He had other plans.

Surgery day was August 23, 2020. I was prepped and rolled into the theatre. Several hours later, l was moved into the intensive care recovery unit alive, well, coronavirus free, and soon walking! Hallelujah! Glory to God!

"For You have delivered my soul from death, my eyes from tears, and my feet from falling. I will walk before the Lord in the land of the living."

— Psalm 116:8-9, NKJV

This was my turning point. God allowed a series of events that changed my life. He systematically revealed and purged me of false dependencies that led me back to the only true dependency: God, my Rock and my Salvation.

During medical treatments, He gave me four words affirming His love and promises—you are **Reset**, **Restored**, **Renewed**, and at **Rest**. Then, God started His surgery and, by His grace, my healing journey to His place of Rest began with a **Reset**.

Chapter 1
RESET

re·set pronounced (ˌ)rē-ˈset: to set
again or anew.

I n the book of Acts of the Apostles 9:1-20,[1] (New Living
Translation) the Bible records the events that led to
Saul's, also known as Paul's,[2] conversion to Christianity. On
his journey to Damascus, Jesus revealed Himself to Paul
dramatically and took away his sight. After this revelation,
Paul was moved to *reflect* on his life, *release* his previous
beliefs, and *repent*. His obedient response to Jesus after the
encounter led him to regaining his sight, being baptised by
the Holy Spirit, and doing mighty exploits for the Kingdom
of God. God **Reset**[3] his vision, purpose, and life.

Like the apostle Paul, we will all meet or experience a "Damascus" moment when God stops us in our tracks. I gave
details of my "Damascus" moment in the prologue. The
moment should not be ignored but, instead, embraced as an
opportunity for positive change.

It is a privilege to be reset by God, the loving Almighty
Father. Only some are fortunate enough to be corrected or
re-directed by a loving father. It may not be as dramatic as

Paul's experience or as life-threatening as mine, but it could be a subtle sign or push in the right direction.

Hebrews 12:5-7 says, *"And have you forgotten the encouraging words God spoke to you as his children? He said, 'My child, don't make light of the Lord's discipline, and don't give up when he corrects you. For the Lord disciplines those he loves, and he punishes each one he accepts as his child. As you endure this divine discipline, remember that God is treating you as his own children. Who ever heard of a child who is never disciplined by its father?'"*[4]

Much like an earthly parent or guardian, when subtlety doesn't work, the corrective approach is amplified to get our attention. Our response to God's chastisement and pruning is essential. When it happens, what will we do with it? Will we ignore it or give in to the opportunity to reset our lives?

The events in 2020 forced me to *reflect, release,* and *repent,* which opened the door to God's revelation concerning my life and reset. As seen in the illustration in the prologue, I carried a myriad of life complexities, issues, and burdens. I was sick physically but also fractured spiritually. In the process of reflecting, I found my identity in Christ, and that is, and will always be, enough. My **Reset** began with my ***spirit***.

Reflect

Reset without spiritual reflection and a revelation of our true self through God's lens will not be successful.

"Only God can reveal the truth about our identity."

When this truth is revealed, we realise how far we are from God's original blueprint for our lives, which is always better than the path we create for ourselves. The reflection of God's blueprint, the best plan, should trigger a yearning to get back on track and be transformed into His image.

> *"But we all, with unveiled face, beholding as in a mirror the glory of the Lord, are being transformed into the same image from glory to glory, just as by the Spirit of the Lord."*
>
> — 2 Corinthians 3:18, NKJV

Over the course of my life, I have moved houses at least five times. Moving prompted me to clean up, which I did by organising my belongings into keep, giveaway, and junk boxes.

"Create room for a fresh new start."

I learnt to keep only what I needed for my new home and let the others go into respective boxes. The giveaway box revealed that some things no longer had a place in my life or were misplaced and better served as a blessing to others. The junk box revealed that I was holding on to things that were either not intended for me or were no longer useful in my life. The junk box was waste that occupied space.

With each move, the sorting process got easier. The experience left me feeling lighter, so I got bolder with my selections and looked forward to creating room for a fresh new start; however, despite my attempts, some items seemed to get into the keep box that didn't belong there. They became excess baggage.

"Reflect, then release the excess toxic baggage to God."

Whenever I chose to carry excess baggage into a new house, it ended up as junk waste. Waste occupies space and begins gathering dust, harbouring pests and germs, which becomes toxic. Toxicity is an unhealthy condition that breeds sickness and disease. Commercial travel airlines have baggage allowance restrictions. Excess baggage requires a fee. Similarly, carrying extra baggage in life can lead to life-threatening toxicity. Like saving money by not carrying excess baggage onto aeroplanes, I realised the value of moving through life, extra baggage-free. So, I applied the same moving principles to every other aspect of my life. Through reflection, I consciously cleared out the excess toxic baggage —negative thoughts, relationships, possessions, habits, and behaviours, and made adjustments as the years went by. I now travel light and free.

"For you died to this life, and your real life is hidden with Christ in God."

— Colossians 3:3, NLT

Perhaps you, too, are holding onto "excess baggage," which, like all harboured waste, becomes toxic. It is time to set yourself free and travel light.

Reflect, then *release* the baggage to God.

Release

"Unforgiveness breeds and festers cancers"

Releasing yourself and all the toxic baggage begins with forgiveness, a major life changer. Unforgiveness breeds and festers cancers.[5] Forgiving others, circumstances, offences, and, most importantly, forgiving yourself and letting go of regret, sets you free.

Looking at the life of the apostle Paul before his conversion, he was highly knowledgeable and focused on performing his service tasks. He describes himself aptly in Galatians 1:13-14 (NKJV): *"For you have heard of my former conduct in Judaism, how I persecuted the church of God beyond measure and tried to destroy it. And I advanced in Judaism beyond many of my contemporaries in my own nation, being more exceedingly zealous for the traditions of my fathers."* [6]

Similarly, in the story of Mary and Martha, we see Martha also focused on performing her service tasks.

> *"Martha was distracted with much serving, and she approached Him and said, 'Lord, do You not care that my*

sister has left me to serve alone? Therefore, tell her to help
me.' And Jesus answered and said to her, 'Martha, Martha,
you are worried and troubled about many things. But one
thing is needed, and Mary has chosen that good part, which
will not be taken away from her.'"

— Luke 10:40-42, NKJV

Both Paul and Martha were good at serving purposefully for a good cause. They appeared to be performance-driven, unmindful of God's specific time and purpose until their encounters with Jesus Christ pointed them back in the right direction.

"Performance" kept me busy and distracted by serving. I was serving my career, societal standards, and life's expectations. Busy being good at what I did, in my mind, was necessary and for a good cause, but I left out what was most important for the long haul of eternity, God's specific purpose for me, until I was stopped.

Having lost my father at a young age, I was raised by my mother and siblings. Being the youngest had its privileges and downsides. It shielded me, allowing me to learn from their lives vicariously, but unfortunately, my position naturally made me the last stop for handed-down household chores. Two potent seeds grew in me as I became old enough to handle chores. First, it became important to me to be independent and not rely on others to get things done. The second was to do my tasks in the order, efficiency, and perfection that did not require a repeat; I genuinely hated being called back to repeat a chore. So, independence, efficiency, and organising became my strongest traits, which later helped me excel in school and at work.

Being performance-driven, I set high standards for myself and was my greatest critic. Though performance, attaining high standards, and pursuing excellence have their place in life and reap many benefits, it eventually took a heavy toll on me. Reflection caused me to dig deep into the source of heaviness. I found that my quest for high performance had worn me out and left me with regret and guilt from past mistakes, failures, and even the smallest of shortcomings.

Dealing with regret was difficult for me, particularly with two significant situations in my life. The first was not staging a life-changing intervention when I had the heart and influence to do so, and the second was making a wrong decision that had a long-term impact on my life.

> *"Letting go of the encumbrance*
> *of regret, by forgiving yourself*
> *and others, sets you free"*

In both situations, God used the circumstances to trigger a revelation of the root cause of some life cancers that I harboured, which led me to Reset in Him.

Not forgiving myself, despite the finished work of Jesus Christ on the cross of Calvary, hindered me from releasing and casting all my cares and burdens upon God. I had to let go of the encumbrance of regret, starting with forgiving myself and others. I had to learn not to be so hard on myself and give myself a break. I had to release myself from seeking validation and working for God's approval through my performance. I did this by believing the Word of God, which says I am forgiven and free.[7]

> *"Therefore, if the Son makes you free, you shall be free indeed."*
>
> — John 8:36, NKJV

If Jesus Christ forgave and forgot my sins,[8] why do I carry regret, guilt, shame, and condemnation, even after confessing my sins and trying to make amends where possible? It was the devil's trap to keep me broken; it was excess baggage. I needed to release the baggage.

> *"For I will be merciful to their unrighteousness, and their sins and their lawless deeds I will remember no more."*
>
> — Hebrews 8:12, NKJV

Unforgiveness doesn't always happen due to the will not to forgive. Sometimes, it gets lost in the layers of our lives and festers, hidden, until it pops up unexpectantly, and you realise you haven't dealt with it. So, what do you do then? Take it back to God in prayer.

"The eternal relevance, reward, and power of God's purpose for our lives far exceed the temporal pain of sickness, disease and unforgiveness."

With God, the fruit of purpose is eternal, and pain is temporal. Be afraid of what can destroy the eternal and let go of that which is temporal.

I thank God for continuously forgiving my sins and releasing me of ALL encumbrances. I thank Him for the gift of peace and lightheartedness. What a feeling of freedom! Forgiven, forgiving, releasing all to God, I thank you, Father.

"What a feeling of freedom! Forgiven, forgiving, releasing all to God."

Repent

Perhaps you are carrying excess baggage and seeking a Reset for your life. Initiating self-realisation by *reflection* leads to *release* and genuine *repentance*. Respond to the call of God in obedience. Repentance births humility. Humility is a subject that often comes up in this book.

At the point of humility, we are more open and receptive recipients of God's grace[9] and revelation.

"God loves and accepts us just as we are."

God opened my heart to receive a blueprint of His original design and purpose for my life in the season of my repentance.

He validated this love and forgiveness for me, and my confirmation is the abounding peace and joy I feel in my heart and spirit, despite the ailing circumstances around me.

All these circumstances no longer matter because I made it right with God.

"For God so loved the world that He gave His only begotten Son, that whoever believes in Him should not perish but have everlasting life."

— John 3:16, NKJV

It is God's will for us all to be saved.

"For everyone who calls on the name of the Lord will be saved."

— Romans 10:13, NLT

"This is good and pleases God our Saviour, who wants everyone to be saved and to understand the truth. For, there is one God and one Mediator who can reconcile God and humanity—the man Christ Jesus. He gave his life to purchase freedom for everyone. This is the message God gave to the world at just the right time."

— 1 Timothy 2:3-6, NLT

God requests that we repent, confess our sins, and turn to Him.

"If we confess our sins, He is faithful and just to forgive us our sins and to cleanse us from all unrighteousness."

— 1 John 1:9, NKJV

"God overlooked people's ignorance about these things in earlier times, but now he commands everyone everywhere to repent of their sins and turn to him."

— Acts 17:30, NLT

Remember to Give Thanks

"The blessings and goodness of God consistently surpass our difficulties."

Thanksgiving is the positive attitude of showing gratitude to God by praising and worshipping Him.[10] Remembering the blessings and goodness of God, which consistently surpass our difficulties, should be a recurring posture throughout life. It projects the power of God in our lives. It stirs up our innermost joy, builds contentment, and gives us hope for the future, knowing that the same God who did it before will do it again.

The Bible states that God inhabits the praises of His people,[11] and wherever God is present, ALL situations bow down and align to His power and glory. This is why each prayer in this book begins with a line of thanksgiving to God.

In all things, give thanks to God according to His Word. Never stop giving thanks!

"Always be joyful. Never stop praying. Be thankful in all circumstances, for this is God's will for you who belong to Christ Jesus."

— 1 Thessalonians 5:16-18, NLT

"And give thanks for everything to God the Father in the name of our Lord Jesus Christ."

— Ephesians 5:20, NLT

Embark on your journey by pressing the **Reset** button. Ask God to help you self-*reflect*, *release*, and *repent*. You can begin by saying this simple prayer.

Prayer

Dear God,
Thank You for today and for sustaining my life. I come before You in the spirit of reset and repentance. I confess that I have sinned against You and ask You to forgive me for all my sins. According to Your Word, please cleanse me from all unrighteousness.[12] I accept Jesus Christ as Lord and Saviour over my life and ask Jesus to come into my heart and restore my life. Create in me a clean heart and renew the right spirit within me.[13] Thank You for loving me, saving me, and

answering my prayers. In the name of Jesus Christ, I pray. Amen.

If you said this prayer, congratulations on making the best life decision. For sure, God hears our prayers.[14]

> *"Now this is the confidence that we have in Him, that if we ask anything according to His will, He hears us."*

> — 1 John 5:14, NKJV

Your best life's journey to finding rest in God is here. Your bespoke revelation will come, and in your next chapter, the **Restoration** will begin.

Chapter 2
RESTORE

re·store pronounced ri-'stȯr: give
back, return

We continue to glean from the story of Paul's conversion in the same Bible text.[1] After his encounter with Jesus, his companions led him to Damascus. He remained blind for three days and did not eat or drink.[2] As he was praying, Paul received a vision of his restoration. Just as Jesus had shown him in the vision, he was visited by Ananias, who laid hands on him on the instruction of Jesus, and instantly Paul's sight was restored. Then, Paul got up and was baptised, ate some food, regained his strength, and stayed with believers for a few days before embarking on his mission to preach the gospel of Jesus Christ.[3]

That day, not only was Paul's physical sight **Restored**, but so was his spiritual sight. Through God-purposed visions and Holy Spirit baptism, the trajectory of his life's purpose changed for the better.[4]

Paul took some necessary actions, which we will explore. He prayed and received a vision; he was obedient to accept help from a stranger to regain his sight; he got up and was baptised; he ate food and regained his strength; and then, he tarried with believers before embarking on his journey with a **Renewed** purpose.

His experience demonstrates that **Reset** gives passage to **Restoration.** For restoration to physically flow into being, it primarily requires a spiritual reset—the prayer staple leading to receiving a vision or purposeful direction from God and Holy Spirit baptism; and this, subsequently, leads to physical action.

In Chapter One, my **Reset** focused on the spirit, the core of my being that channels deeper connection, experience, and relationship with God. This opened the door for God to **Restore** what I had lost, which was the strength and abilities of my physical **body**. I underwent a restorative process of physical recovery that included *rehabilitation, reliance,* and *relearning.*

"Reset gives passage to Restoration."

Rehabilitation

National Geographic describes the Terracotta Army as one of the "greatest archeological discoveries in the world."[5] The life-sized army was discovered in 1974 by workers digging a well outside the city of Xi'an, China. According to archaeologists, it is part of an elaborate mausoleum created to accompany China's first Emperor, Qin Shi Huang, into the afterlife. In the 2021 CGTN media story titled "Men of the

People: Restorers bring the terracotta army back to life,"[6] Meng Quinsheng reports "When the life-sized clay figures were unearthed, most of them were damaged or ruined either by natural factors like floods or by human activities. For nearly 50 years, experts have been working to restore life-sized clay figures. The process of repairing a single piece usually takes months or even years to complete."

Consider that if men take so much time, and for some a lifetime, to restore what is deemed valuable on earth, how much more does our Heavenly Father, who knows the number of hairs on our heads,[7] pay keen attention to us, His precious children, concerning every detail of our lives to restore us to Himself?

Has the impact of human and environmental factors, life's activities, and experiences eroded, scarred, or derailed your dreams, purpose, or course in life? Like the Terracotta Army, the damage or ruin is not irreversible; God's restoration is available for you.

Restoration sometimes requires us to go through the process of rehabilitation and repair. The process takes time; for some, longer than others. Mine had strict recovery guidelines and rules that affected my physical senses—*touch, taste, smell, sight*, and *hearing*.

Touch
Rebuild Your Strength

After surgery, I was cold, numb, and immobile. Grateful to be alive but in excruciating pain. Two titanium rods secured by ten pedicle screws were expertly placed in my back, and forty-six staples and several surgical sutures held entrance wounds together. It felt like a ton of bricks was attached to my back. I remember being told that actions in the immediate aftermath of surgery determine the success of the surgery. For me, that meant the ability to walk and function optimally depended not only on my faith in God but also on my actions. From here on, my actions were my choice, no one else's. I chose to walk and live, so I had to make an effort and take action.

As part of my rehabilitation process, I had over 50 prescribed physiotherapy sessions and tailored exercises incorporated into my daily routine. Missed or incorrectly performed exercises could alter the reconstructive work that had been done and hinder my mobility. But continued sessions improved my strength, flexibility, and mobility. I gradually regained the ability to feel in the numb areas, my sense of touch returned, and I rebuilt my strength.

Taking care of our bodies is essential to living a fulfilling life and is a sign of respect and appreciation to God, our Creator.[8]

> *"Or do you not know that your body is the temple of the Holy Spirit who is in you, whom you have from God, and you are not your own? For you were bought at a price; therefore, glorify God in your body and in your spirit, which are God's."*

> — 1 Corinthians 6:19-20, NKJV

We cannot adequately care for our bodies or do the work necessary to restore them without the help of our God, who created them. In the apostle Paul's letter to Timothy, he instructs that *"Physical training is good, but training for godliness is much better, promising benefits in this life and in the life to come"* (1 Timothy 4: 8, NLT). [9]

The benefits of godliness include recognising the complete work of Christ's death on the cross, who we are in Him, and holding on to His promises concerning our redemption, health, and restoration.

Here are four verses that keep me strong in the difficulty of my physical rehabilitation.

I hope they also inspire you to keep going, no matter the circumstances.

"Do not be afraid; only believe."

— Mark 5:36b (NKJV)

"Surely He has borne our griefs and carried our sorrows; ... He was wounded for our transgressions, He was bruised for our iniquities; The chastisement for our peace was upon Him, and by His stripes we are healed."

— Isaiah 53:4a-5, NKJV

"The Sovereign Lord is my strength! He makes me as sure-footed as a deer, able to tread upon the heights."

— Habakkuk 3:19, NLT

"...be strong in the Lord and in the power of His might."

— Ephesians 6:10, NKJV

Taste and Smell
Feed Your Body to Preserve Your Body

Daily combinations of different medications took a toll that altered my tastebuds and heightened my sense of smell, which led to nausea. Eating food was no longer a favourite past time and neither was drinking water. But without eating the right food and drinking enough water, I couldn't be administered most of my medications, so I had to find the will to get up, eat, and drink to receive my medications.

My diet had to change to nourish, heal, and preserve my body, sustainably and healthily. With the help of a nutritionist, I found that some of my favourite foods were good for my body, but most were doing more harm than good, so they were no longer acceptable.

"All things are lawful for me, but all things are not helpful. All things are lawful for me, but I will not be brought under the power of any."

— 1 Corinthians 6:12, NKJV

So, I learnt to approach food not with a sense of deprivation but with the consciousness of feeding my body to support its preservation.

"Therefore, whether you eat or drink, or whatever you do, do all to the glory of God."

— 1 Corinthians 10: 31, NKJV

Sight and Hearing
Guard Your Heart. Fuel and Ignite Your Spirit.

Have you ever wondered why, when you hear a song or watch a video repetitively, it unconsciously plays back in your mind throughout the day? I thought about this and found some research and theory on human memory. The Harvard University Derek Bok Center for Teaching and Learning defines memory as "the ongoing process of information retention over time. It is an integral part of human cognition since it allows individuals to recall and draw upon past events to frame their understanding of and behaviour within the present."[10]

Translating this to my experience, I established that what I continuously hear and see, good or bad, is retained and recalled in my brain as memories. My memories frame my perception, thoughts, reasoning, understanding, and behaviour. Therefore, whatever I choose to feed my eyes and ears has a residual impact and influence on my heart and life.

"Approach food not with a sense of deprivation but with the consciousness of feeding your body to support its preservation."

This enlightened my interpretation of the Bible verse that advises us "to guard our hearts above all else, for it determines the course of our life."[11] The course of our life includes the choices we make concerning our health and well-being.

Being selective about what and who has access to my ears (what I hear) and eyes (what I see) helped me tremendously. Technology gives us access to a colourful myriad of good and bad content. But thankfully, it also offers the ability to switch off negative voices, images, and messages with a simple touch button or finger swipe. No matter how tempting, I had the choice and tools to efficiently and consistently filter my content to keep negativity, the life cancers that try to infiltrate my life, out.

But what fills the vacuum? An intentional selection of positive sights and sounds. I prioritize activities that bring me joy and laughter, such as listening to music, dancing, and visual art. In Chapter Four, I further elaborate on my experience with positive content.

It was easy to control the physical things. But the devil doesn't only strike physically; he attacks mentally and emotionally too. The deep hidden places of the heart and mind do not have a button to switch off and on. But God gave me the remedy for that by helping me retain His Word in my heart and mind through prayer, praise, and worship.

Exercising my body daily restored my strength, as did exercising my spirit. Declaring my rights as a child of God ignites the power of God that tears down all strongholds and territories that defied my healing process. By praying daily and feeding my ears, eyes and, thus, my heart with the Word of God, partaking of the holy communion, and using the Word of God to respond to every situation, I shut down the negative voices of death and anything contrary to the promises of God concerning my life.

The devil does not play fair and wait for you to stand up before throwing punches. In my darkest and weakest hours, I still received bad news, personal attacks, and physical challenges that floated in whispers of doubt, death, and fear.

But Hallelujah! The Word of God has power,[12] and the name of Jesus Christ is above every other name! Every knee bows down at the mention of the name of Jesus![13]

Glory to God! What a mighty God we serve!

> "Therefore God also has highly exalted Him and given Him the name which is above every name, that at the name of Jesus every knee should bow, of those in heaven, and of those on earth, and of those under the earth, and that every tongue should confess that Jesus Christ is Lord, to the glory of God the Father."
>
> — Philippians 2:9-11, NKJV

In the battlefield of my mind and spirit, I speak the Word of God in the name of Jesus to the situation and stand leaning in on the Word with every breath until peace flows in my heart. It always does because the Word of God never fails.[14]

"Every word of God is pure; He is a shield to those who put their trust in Him."

— Proverbs 30:5, NKJV

For these reasons, all the prayers in this book are rooted in the Word of God. Speak the Word in the good times and the bad. Speak the Word as your daily affirmations. Stay in the Word of God and surround yourself with positive sights and sounds—music, messages, content, people, etc.

Praising and worshipping God is also part of a Christian's instruments of war. When we fill our hearts and mouths with songs of praise to God, it triggers His presence in our situation and infuses God's medicinal peace and joy into our hearts.

"A cheerful heart is good medicine, but a broken spirit saps a person's strength."

— Proverbs 17:22, NLT

Reliance

"Trusting that God was in control of the people and process makes decisions easy."

Being in the hospital is a humbling experience. You are frequently exposed to the human body's frailty with heart-breaking cries of pain, loss and death. There are no touch buttons to shut out this reality. It elevates humanity's weakness, offering teachable moments to reflect on your life. It clarifies that everyone needs someone who will love, support, and be kind to or care for us at some point. We will all rely on another human being in life and even death. Therefore, forging genuine human relationships in life is beneficial to all. I share more about my experience with relationships in Chapter Four.

Like the apostle Paul, my condition had placed me in a location and situation that was out of my control. I was unable, and often not permitted, to make medical decisions. This often left me at the mercy of experts and caregivers who were mostly strangers. In Paul's case, the strangers were Ananias and the disciples and, in mine, doctors, nurses, and medical personnel.

Sometimes receiving help and trusting others with your life is hard, particularly when life has dished you a catalogue of bad experiences. But I had to either give in to the healing process or deal with adverse consequences. Trusting that God was in control of the people and process made the decision easy. I humbly gave in, became open and receptive to medical instructions, and became obedient to those assigned to ensure that my recovery went smoothly.

I am grateful to God for my husband, who stood by me every step of the way, making tough calls and decisions when I was in and out of consciousness. He was holding fort to ensure I was in the right place and time to receive treatment. But, at a point, he also had to let go of control, rely on the experts, and trust God for a positive outcome.

The Bible doesn't say all that Paul did during his time with the disciples. But I assume he was being cared for, unlearning and relearning from "expert or experienced" strangers before starting his journey. He lived and, therefore, had to build relationships with the people he was persecuting. In a similar way, we can never determine whose hands our life may depend on during our respective journeys.

As I mentioned, we will all rely on another human being at some point. This brings to question how we treat those God has placed in our lives to help us. How do we treat our family, friends, colleagues, staff, neighbours, caregivers, peers, and strangers? Are we kind, receptive, and thankful? How do we express gratitude to those who love, trust, support, sacrifice, and appreciate us? Do we value and prioritise them with a show of love in ways that they understand and appreciate? If not, consider doing so as led by the *most reliable* God, our Father.

Relearning

Healing was challenging, but dependence and losing control of what you do as a routine is also tricky and humbling. The illustration before the prologue indicates the weight of the medical procedures, burdens, and experiences I carried; however, my faith in God gave me the right attitude and disposition to create an atmosphere of gratitude. This made me better able to receive the knowledge and help I needed to understand my disability while vulnerably recognising my fears so that I could overcome them. Then I began to relearn.

Relearning requires patience and expertise to ensure it is done well and retained. I was fortunate to have a caring team of medical personnel and caregivers whom I relied on for help, personal care, medical care, and support systems.

They helped me relearn how to walk, sit up, and lie down with the correct posture and educated me on work/home modifications and healthy habits to imbibe. I fell and failed many times, but God gave me courage and surrounded me with a cheering team that helped me get back up and try again. Slowly, I regained my independence and learnt to restore good habits, severe toxic ones, and create new sustainable ones.

"Work hard to show the results of your salvation, obeying God with deep reverence and fear."

— Philippians 2:12b, NLT

I cannot imagine the outcome of my stay during this critical recovery time in the hospital if God had not placed the right people in the right place and at the right time to support my health journey. I am grateful to God for the opportunity He gave me to know and personally thank them for their care and professionalism.

"Restore good habits, severe toxic ones and create new sustainable ones."

Restoration requires effort, work, and discipline. It can be painful, and sometimes a long and winding road, but we reach the expected end victoriously with God. God has given us a spirit of power,[15] love, and self-discipline.[16] He promises to restore, confirm, strengthen, and establish us.[17] He restores and returns better than what we've had or been before.

> *"In his kindness God called you to share in his eternal glory by means of Christ Jesus. So, after you have suffered a little while, he will restore, support, and strengthen you, and he will place you on a firm foundation."*
>
> — 1 Peter 5:10, NLT

As with most things built to last, we must undergo a process. Our journey with God is as unique and individual as our DNA. Don't be hard on yourself; give into the process. Remember to stay humble[18] to learn, patient to listen, hungry to heal, and always give thanks, then watch God restore you and take you into **Renewal**.

> ***"Restoration requires effort,***
> ***work, and discipline."***

> ***"Stay humble to learn, patient to listen,***
> ***hungry to heal and always give thanks."***

Prayer

Dear God, my Father,
Thank You for receiving me as Your child and promising to restore, support, strengthen, and place me on a firm foundation.[19] I recognise that I need You to heal every part of my life and ask today that You please put me back on the original path and purpose You designed for me. Heal me from all sicknesses and diseases in my spirit, body, and soul. Save me from my wounds and brokenness, for I know that, according to your Word, O Lord, if You heal me, I will be truly healed; if You save me, I will be saved.[20] Restore to me the joy of Your salvation and make me willing to obey You.[21] Please help me to recognise, accept, and appreciate the process and people You place in my life for my complete restoration. Thank You for restoring my health and healing my wounds.[22] In the name of Jesus Christ, I pray. Amen.

The G.R.O.A.T – Greatest Relationship of All Time

"Your journey with God is as unique and individual as your DNA."

Are you facing a situation that seems to have crippled your body and physical senses? Hindered your ability to *feel* the warmth of the sun ushering in a new day, *hear* the joy of your heart's laughter, *see* the bright hope of the future, *taste* the goodness of God, *smell* the blossoming flowers of victory, or *sing* songs of thanksgiving and praise? Has your strength failed? Have you lost all hope due to life's cancers in and around your life and seek restoration?

If yes, you are not alone. Don't give up. There is hope for Restoration, but you cannot do it alone; you need help.

In addition to accepting Jesus Christ as our Lord and Saviour, getting restored requires actions that effectively sustain the ground we have acquired through prayer. An essential step is receiving help and instruction from the Holy Spirit. How? By simply asking God.

In the book of Luke, Jesus Christ teaches us how to pray[23] and tells us that God, the Father, gives the Holy Spirit to those who ask Him. He assures us that, for everyone who asks, receives; who seeks, finds; and who knocks, the door will be opened.[24]

The Holy Spirit is the Spirit of truth that dwells in all of God's children[25] and joins with our spirit to affirm that we are children of God.[26] The Holy Spirit is the Comforter[27] who guides us into all truth[28] and our **Reset**. The Spirit of God, who raised Jesus from the dead, lives within us and gives life to our mortal bodies.[29] The Holy Spirit produces the fruits of love, joy, peace, patience, kindness, goodness, faithfulness, gentleness, and self-control in our lives.[30]

Before His ascension, Jesus highlighted the importance of the baptism of the Holy Spirit by instructing the disciples to remain in Jerusalem till they were baptised by the Holy Spirit.[31] This direction and His instruction to Ananias to baptise Paul,[32] before he embarked on his apostolic commission, indicate the importance for us to ask for and receive the Holy Spirit baptism.

The most significant relationship to have is with the Holy Spirit. The most trustworthy voice to rely on is the Holy Spirit. There is no better helper, guide, or comforter. The Spirit of God sees the innermost parts of our hearts and understands our fears and pain; all we need to do is receive Him, and He will give us the power to do all that is required to live a God-purposed life. If you choose to, you can say this prayer.

> *"The most significant relationship and trustworthy voice is the Holy Spirit. There is no better life helper, guide, or comforter than the Holy Spirit"*

Prayer

Dear God,
Thank You for the gift of the Holy Spirit. I give You
full access to my heart and life and ask You to baptise
me with Your Holy Spirit. Pour into me and fill me
with Your power, with the evidence of the gift of
speaking in tongues[33] *and with the fruits of Your*
spirit[34]—*love, joy, peace, patience, kindness, goodness,*
faithfulness, gentleness, and self-control. For this, I
pray, believe, and receive in the name of Jesus Christ.
Amen.

To learn more about receiving baptism and understanding the advantages of the Holy Spirit, please refer to the Healing Resources section at the end of the book.

Chapter 3
RENEW

re·new pronounced ri-'nü -'nyü: to
make like new

The parables of Jesus are some of the most profound messages in the Bible. Each parable allows me to immerse myself within its lines, experience the wisdom of Jesus Christ, and learn from His lessons.

In Luke 5:36-38 (NKJV), Jesus Christ used a parable to respond to an enquiry about the actions of His disciples, saying: *"No one puts a piece from a new garment on an old one; otherwise, the new makes a tear, and also the piece that was taken out of the new does not match the old. And no one puts new wine into old wineskins, or else the new wine will burst the wineskins and be spilled, and the wineskins will be ruined. But new wine must be put into new wineskins, and both are preserved."*[1]

To better comprehend this text, I dug deeper into the wine-making process and the use of wineskins as a container.

A wineskin is an ancient type of bottle made of leathered animal skin, usually from goats or sheep, used to store or transport wine.[2] In their paper titled, "Why wineskins? In the exploration of a relationship between wine and skin containers," Barbara Wills and Amanda Watts describe the process of ancient winemaking. "Wine was typically made by the extraction of the grape juice followed by initial fermentation in a large container. During fermentation, sugar converts to alcohol by the action of yeast, and in warm climates, this proceeds quickly and unavoidably. The exothermic reaction produces carbon dioxide, pressurising a container unless allowed to escape."[3]

Chris Hartenstein also illustrates the ancient process of making wine through fermentation or ageing wine in his April 7th, 2020 post titled, "New Wine, Old Wineskins." He says, "Because the wineskin was new, it could expand and hold both the wine and the gasses; however, if someone poured unfermented juice into an old wineskin, the forming gasses caused the skin to burst. As a result, they lost both the new wine and old wineskin."[4]

Understanding the ancient winemaking process gave me personal insight into the related parable. It reveals that a new life, operating in old conditions, destroys the new and the old. Conversely, a new life operating in new conditions preserves both.

In previous chapters, I describe the process of Reset and Restoration, which aligned my spirit and body with God's purpose and plan. God carried me through victoriously, and I bear the battle scars like decorative stripes to prove it. Progress has been made, and I have gained ground. My spirit is Reset, and my body is Restored. Hallelujah! I am a new creation! My old self has passed away, and the new me has come.[5]

> "Therefore, if anyone is in Christ, he is a new creation; old things have passed away; behold, all things have become new."

— 2 Corinthians 5:17, NKJV

But shall I continue in the sins of my past so that God's abundant grace abounds? No![6]

> "Well then, should we keep on sinning so that God can show us more and more of his wonderful grace? Of course not! Since we have died to sin, how can we continue to live in it? Or have you forgotten that when we were joined with Christ Jesus in baptism, we joined him in his death? For we died and were buried with Christ by baptism. And just as Christ was raised from the dead by the glorious power of the Father, now we also may live new lives."

— Romans 6:1-3, NLT

My old wineskins and garments have been traded for new wineskins and garments; however, to receive and preserve the outpouring of God's new wine into my life, I needed to prepare my new skin and garments by **Renew**ing my mind.[7]

"And be renewed in the spirit of your mind, and that you put on the new man which was created according to God, in true righteousness and holiness."

— Ephesians 4:22-24, NKJV

I prepared using *records*, *restructuring*, and *reform*.

Records

The Bible is a collection of spirit-led, life-changing records from God. I shudder to think where we would be if the lessons, stories, and encounters in the Bible were not recorded or preserved.

I began journaling early, as a teenager, but more intensely, purposely, and productively when I re-dedicated my life to Christ. It started with writing and drawing my thoughts in poetry and art illustration. As I grew older, this practice evolved to taking notes at church services, documenting my prayer requests and testimonies, and transcribing sermons through the eyes of my understanding as I sought answers to life's challenges. These notes became my *spiritual "records"* and serve as points of reference, evidence, and a reminder that God is with me, particularly in difficult times. My journey's scars and written testimonies prove that I went through significantly painful experiences but made it through alive. They continuously **Renew** my mind from doubt and fear. I expand more on my experience with fear at the end of this chapter.

Issues in life often come unannounced, and it's easy to forget God's victories by putting a spotlight on what's going wrong. When I am not anchored by a renewed mind, packed with the memories of God's Word, His promises and His spotless reputation of unmatched victory over the devil, I waver in battle.

> *"But thanks be to God, who gives us the victory through our Lord Jesus Christ!"*
>
> — 1 Corinthians 15:57, NKJV

While in the hospital for surgery, the importance of keeping records in my mind came into play. Having limited accessibility and control of my environment, I relied entirely on my memories to get me through unconsciousness, nights, and cold chilling sounds reverberating from the rooms and corridors. I thank God for the moments when Bible verses, His track record of testimonies, and songs of praise and worship got engraved in my memory by repetitive use. These bubbled up in my mind, gave me hope for the future, and took me through recovery. So did the *illustration of my vision* for the future.

"Vision is an essential factor in the Renewal process."

Vision[8] is an essential factor in the Renewal process. Sometimes, a vision is given to us directly from God or passed on by a higher influence. Nonetheless, with the help of the

Holy Spirit, personal vision can be created by using our imagination[9] to form mental images in our minds. A vision is best retained and preserved when brought to life in writing or visual illustration, transforming it into a tangible and replicable *record*.

> *"Then the Lord answered me and said: 'Write the vision and make it plain on tablets, that he may run who reads it. For the vision is yet for an appointed time, but at the end it will speak, and it will not lie. Though it tarries, wait for it; Because it will surely come, it will not tarry.'"*
>
> — Habakkuk 2:2-3, NKJV

In the prologue, I mentioned arranging for my photos to be taken before surgery as a memorial for my children. I remember imagining, writing, and creating a vision of what I would look like in total and perfect health, joy, and peace. At the time, I didn't know that God intended it to be a record that renewed my mind during recovery.

When I met the blessed and talented photographer, T. Y. Bello, and shared my ideas for the photo shoot , I was in the most intense physical pain my body had ever experienced and at the peak of sickness and despondency. I could barely sit up without support, but God miraculously fuelled my purpose and strengthened me. In hindsight, what I experienced that day was the hand of God working through every person on the set to bring life to this testimony. The photos I saw in the camera preview brought tears to my eyes. God put a smile on my face, a glint in my eyes, and joy in my step.

They expressed more than my words could describe, far better than what I imagined. The images left an embeddable mark in my memory. They became *the record of my vision* that gave me hope and focus for better days ahead. Visual records helped me through my physical **Restoration** and preserved me in my **Renewed** state. Glory to God!

For this reason, I chose to include the photos in this book to show the power of God's healing grace and mercy. The images are a product of faith, showing "the reality of what I hoped for and the evidence of things I could not see,"[10] which have now come to pass, are seen, and are being experienced. This is the power of recorded vision.

> *"And we know that God causes everything to work together for the good of those who love God and are called according to his purpose for them."*

> — Romans 8:28, NLT

I encourage you to document your journey with God. Keep and mark them as records in your heart; preserve them in your mind. As stated in Chapter Two, memory is enhanced by repetition. Form good habits of counteracting life's issues by reading, speaking, and replaying the Word of God, so it is embedded in your memory.

As every individual's circumstances differ, it's necessary to say that not all records should be retained. Records that fuel toxicity in your life should be handled cautiously, according to God's purpose and leading. In Chapter One, I described my process for releasing excess baggage, including toxicity, by grouping them into keep, giveaway, or junk boxes. My indicator for good record management is the sense of deep peace after deciding how to handle them. Ask God to help you categorise and manage your records.

This book is the product of two decades of unscripted conversations and experiences with God. I am grateful to God that I started keeping records early, but it's never too late for you to start.

> ***"Where there is no order, there is chaos.***
> ***Where there is chaos, there is no peace;***
> ***where there is no peace, there is no <u>Rest</u>."***

God operates in order and with intention. The Bible is packed with many examples of God's successive works of order, every purposeful stitch meshing in the beautiful tapestry of His excellent grand design for our redemption. From His creation of the heavens, the earth, and the perfect balance of time and seasons in the book of Genesis,[11] to His intricate and detailed design of the Holy Tabernacle, priesthood garments and furnishings in the book of Exodus,[12] through to the royal succession plan leading to the birth of Jesus Christ,[13] it is clear to me that God is deliberate, intentional, detailed, and orderly.

I daresay that where there is no order, there is chaos. Where there is chaos, there is no peace; where there is no peace, there is no **Rest**.

As mentioned in Chapter One, being organised is a honed trait that comes to me effortlessly; however, preserving the flow of God's new wine in my life required more than the superficial "labelling of boxes." A deeper layer of order was needed to **Renew** my mind. I did it by *restructuring* and *reforming* it.

Restructure

Insights from the Parable of New and Old Wineskins clarified that trying to fit my old lifestyle into a new one is equal to forcing a "square peg into a round hole."[14] It won't work, and forceful attempts to do so are not only futile but have dire consequences.

Restructuring[15] my mind meant deliberately changing my life patterns and practices to align with God's original intention and purpose for me. It meant *reprioritising* and *repositioning* the place of God in my life by putting Him first in all things.

So, in all situations, I ask myself, "Does this align with God's will and purpose for me?" The answer to this question guides the priority level I place on each task, and this helps me to make decisions based on its position of importance in my life. I put more time into, and pay more attention to, things that fulfil my purpose and little or no time to the things that diminish, distract, or destroy it.

This goes back to understanding our purpose in God, as Chapter One indicates—**Reset**ting and receiving God's purpose and vision for our lives.

Once I received clarity on my purpose, the order of priority for self, family, career, relationships, responsibilities, and barometer for success fell into perfect order. It also provided clarity and ease in making critical choices concerning my well-being and activity in all aspects of my life.

Be it social, political, economic, or communal; our choices should lead to a balanced, peaceful, fulfilled life that keeps us connected with God.

Reform

To reform means to put or change into an improved form or condition.[16]

> ***"The Word of God, the Bible, is the
> ultimate tool for reforming the mind."***

Every day presents a free flow of information, loaded with human opinions, world views, and "facts" that directly or indirectly influence our perspectives and impact our lives.

Looking at this from my restructuring perspective meant that I needed to understand the importance of how I started my day, including my first thoughts and actions, so that I would be better able to control what I automatically fed my mind, giving top priority to what God needed me to do. As I reflected on my morning habits, this became a daunting thought. So daunting, in fact, that I almost knocked off the idea in self-denial until I noticed the impact and stark difference that starting my day with positive versus negative words had on my mood and productivity. It became apparent that whatever information I choose to start my day with feeds, influences, and sets my mind for the course of my day.

Understanding the power and influence that the first line of information has on my mind and my life highlighted the need to *reform* and improve the condition of my mind by monitoring the information that flows into it. Prioritising God meant putting Him first by deliberately seeking His opinion, truth, and view first every day.

Reading and prioritising the Word of God consistently reforms my mind with the truth[17] and enforces God's order, the highest judgement, in any situation I face throughout the day.

"The entirety of Your word is truth, and every one of Your righteous judgments endures forever."

— Psalm 119:160, NKJV

"The Word of God is my first defence against life's cancers."

It counteracts worldly "facts" with God's truth. It's the barrier and filter from all the information that comes through my spirit, body, and mind, sifting out the devil's lies and permitting only God's truth to permeate and settle in my heart and mind. The Word of God reforms me.

Its power provides an effective armoury[18] and courses of action to thrive in a **Renew**ed life.

"For the weapons of our warfare are not carnal but mighty in God for pulling down strongholds, casting down arguments and every high thing that exalts itself against the knowledge of God, bringing every thought into captivity to the obedience of Christ."

— 2 Corinthians 10:4-5, NKJV

The Word of God should take top priority over any other word spoken into our lives and registered in our minds. It is our lifeline.

"For the word of God is alive and powerful. It is sharper than the sharpest two-edged sword, cutting between soul and spirit, between joint and marrow. It exposes our innermost thoughts and desires."

— Hebrews 4:12, NLT

Reforming our minds with God's Word adjusts our will and actions to preserve and maintain the gains achieved by our Reset and Restoration.

I pray that, thus far, you have tasted the goodness of God and experienced His mercy, abundant love, and sovereign power.

Your spirit is Reset; your body is Restored; your mind is Renewed; now, get ready to **Rest**.

Prayer

Dear God,
Thank You for another chance to come before You. I
desire to preserve Your righteousness and holiness[19]
in me and ask that You teach and help me to learn to
do Your perfect, sound, and pleasing will[20] *every day*
of my life. Please guide me through the areas of my life
that need adjustments. Restructure and reform my
life to the order that You purposed for me. Renew my
mind and help me create memorial records of my
journey with You for Your glory. Thank You for trans-
forming my life. In the name of Jesus Christ, I pray.
Amen.

Fear "Tsoro" ...the Mosquito in My Nest

Malaria[21] is a life-threatening disease transmitted to humans through the bites of infected female *Anopheles* mosquitoes. These mosquitoes are predominantly found in tropical regions, including my country of origin, Nigeria, West Africa.

I specifically come from Plateau State, situated in the North Central region of Nigeria.[22] It's known for its beautiful flatlands, vibrant culture, rich soil, mouth-watering fruits and vegetables, valuable minerals, pleasant weather, hospitable people, and breathtaking scenery. But regrettably, just like in the neighbouring states and countries, mosquitoes are prevalent in this area.

Mosquito bites are not only painful but also itchy and uncomfortable. Although preventable and treatable, the anopheles bite is feared because it transmits a disease that has a high fatality rate. According to the World Health Organisation, "the estimated number of malaria deaths stood at 619,000 in 2021."[23]

As a result, I was taught at a young age how to protect myself from mosquito bites. This involved using insecticide, wearing protective clothing, staying within the safety of mosquito nets,[24] avoiding areas where they breed, and taking necessary measures such as preventive, palliative, or curative medicines to ward off infection.

"Tsoro"[25] is the term used for **fear** in the Hausa language, predominantly spoken by many in Nigeria's North Central region. In my personal experience, I have found that fear, or "tsoro," can be compared to a mosquito. This analogy came to me when I faced dreadful medical and life situations. God helped me realise that my experience with protecting myself from mosquito bites could help me overcome a terrible encounter with fear and come out stronger on the other side.

In 2021, I received the most devastating news that left me in despair, brokenness, and filled with FEAR. I rocked back and forth, shaken to my core in confusion, afraid of the uncertain impact this news would have on my life. I could hardly breathe or sleep from the torment of the unfolding events. Feeling vulnerable and scared, I desperately cried to God for help and guidance, but it felt like there was no answer. Eventually, I became exhausted and drifted off into restless sleep.

Shortly after, I was woken up by the persistent sound of a mosquito. I quickly switched on my bedside fan and waved my hand to shoo it away, but the buzzing continued loudly. What was odd, however, was that, despite the mosquito's proximity and loud noise, I didn't feel a bite or any physical contact, just the constant buzzing and movement around me.

Trying to salvage what was left of my sleep, I switched on a soft light to locate it. Sure enough, I saw the mosquito struggling to get through the bed's protective net. Thankfully, I had double-checked for possible openings and tucked in loose ends. So as much as it tried to pass through, my fortress-like net was impenetrable. I felt relieved, but still unsettled, by the annoying buzzing sounds.

I attempted to swat the mosquito, and it vanished. Assuming I had succeeded in terminating it, I settled back under my covers. A little while later, I heard the buzzing sounds again which, this time, appeared closer. In frustration, I shone my flashlight on the mosquito and, to my surprise, it disappeared against the net, casting a looming shadow on the ceiling that made it appear much more significant than it was. It persisted for a while longer before eventually flying away.

Before leaving my bed, I securely closed the net to prevent mosquitoes from entering. Upon my return, I could still hear the mosquitos buzzing around me. I was able to shoo them away, but one flew so close to me that I couldn't resist the chance to kill it. With one swift strike, I hit my target victoriously before quickly and carefully snuggling back into my comfortable space to Rest.

In that moment of rest and reflection, I was comforted by a sense of enlightenment, knowing God had answered my prayer with the following three valuable lessons.

1. My efforts to combat the mosquitos were unnecessary, misguided and, ultimately, futile because I was already under the protection of the mosquito net.
2. Whenever I focused on the tiny mosquito, it seemed to grow and loom, creating a shadow larger than life and distracting me from its true nature. Following the natural cycle of life and death, insects like these generally have a short life span. Without interference, only a small percentage of adult female anopheles mosquitoes live long enough (more than ten days in tropical areas) to spread malaria.[26]

3. Even when I leave the security of my mosquito net,
   I have God-given tools to defend myself.

As with the mosquitos, I spent a lot of effort and resources, as
well as physical, mental, and spiritual energy fighting fear,
but I know better now.

1. God has already protected me. This is a reassuring
realisation. As a child of God, I dwell in His secret
place, under His shadow and wings. He fortifies me,
and no weapon formed against me shall prosper.[27]
Even when my enemies rise against me, they will
fall.[28] God conceals me when troubles come, and He
hides me in His sanctuary, placing me out of reach
on a high rock. [29]

*"'No weapon formed against you shall prosper, and every
tongue which rises against you in judgment, You shall
condemn. This is the heritage of the servants of the Lord,
and their righteousness is from Me,' Says the Lord."*

— Isaiah 54:17, NKJV

*"When evil people come to devour me, when my enemies
and foes attack me, they will stumble and fall. ... For he will
conceal me there when troubles come; He will hide me in
his sanctuary. He will place me out of reach on a high
rock."*

— Psalm 27:2, 5, NLT

2. When I turn my focus to God, my worries and fears begin to fade away. The source of all light[30] and peace grants me rest[31] and fights my battles[32] on my behalf.

"The Lord is my light and my salvation—so why should I be afraid? The Lord is my fortress, protecting me from danger, so why should I tremble?"

— Psalm 27:1, NLT

"I will both lie down in peace, and sleep; For You alone, O Lord, make me dwell in safety."

— Psalm 4:8, NKJV

"The Lord will fight for you, and you shall hold your peace."

— Exodus 14:14, NKJV

3. God clothes me in His armour to stand my ground on the evil day.[33]

"Put on all of God's armour so that you will be able to stand firm against all strategies of the devil."

— Ephesians 6:11-18, NLT

Have you ever found yourself in a state of fear that made you question your faith in God? Or have you experienced persistent, unsettling feelings that distract you from your life's true purpose, like a mosquito buzzing in your ear? This could be due to anxiety, illness, shame, hopelessness, betrayal, or loss. If so, where do you go, or what do you do to overcome it? Have you considered a permanent solution to overcoming fear and the quality of the place you seek refuge from fear?

It is of utmost importance to prioritise and prepare for the imminent battle with fear that life throws at us. We need to prevent fear from taking over and causing harm in our lives. Just like festering mosquitoes, please remember that:

- Fear has no power over us unless we allow it to enter our lives. It is a destructive force that can disrupt our peace and well-being, and it often collaborates with other negative emotions to cause harm.
- Fear can be tricky, difficult to detect, and is often amplified in noise and shadows, making it seem bigger and more significant than it is; however, we can rely on God's light to overcome it.
- Fear needs a suitable environment to grow and can manifest in various forms. It lays dormant until it's ready to strike. Nonetheless, fear is not permanent and will always be defeated by our response of faith.
- Fear can be a natural response to specific situations, acting as a warning sign that something may be wrong. Therefore, we must remain alert. Though fear can be a beneficial survival instinct, it can also be harmful if we allow it to control us.

- We can find comfort in God's perfect love, which eliminates fear.[34]

"And we have known and believed the love that God has for us. God is love, and he who abides in love abides in God, and God in him. Love has been perfected among us in this: that we may have boldness in the day of judgment; because as He is, so are we in this world. There is no fear in love; but perfect love casts out fear because fear involves torment. But he who fears has not been made perfect in love."

— 1 John 4:16-18, NKJV

As for me, I seek refuge from fear in God Almighty, my Father. It is in running to Him that I find true safety. My security lies solely in the redemptive blood of Jesus Christ, [35] and I find an abundance of peace, comfort, and protection in Him for He saves me from destruction.[36]

"He redeems me from death and crowns me with love and tender mercies."

— Psalm 103:4, NLT

You, too, can experience His blanket of security by saying this short prayer.

"My security lies solely in the redemptive blood of Jesus Christ."

Prayer

Dear God,
Thank You for being my place of refuge from fear.[37]
Please help me to focus on You whenever I am afraid
by trading in my fears with faith in Your Word. Teach
me to trust in You so that I can conquer my fears and
emerge victorious in all my battles. In the name of
Jesus Christ, I pray. Amen.

Chapter 4
REST

rest pronounced 'rest: peace of
mind or spirit: freedom from
activity or labour

The Merriam-Webster dictionary defines grace as a
virtue from God, unmerited divine assistance given to
us for our sanctification.[1] It further describes grace as a
special favour, approval, mercy, pardon, clemency, privilege,
or an act of kindness.

God's grace is a gift bestowed on us for free.[2] By His grace,
we are saved through the finished work of Jesus Christ on the
Cross of Calvary and made righteous[3] at the point of our
salvation.

> *"God saved you by His grace when you believed. And you*
> *can't take credit for this; it is a gift from God. Salvation is*
> *not a reward for the good things we have done, so none of us*
> *can boast about it. For we are God's masterpiece. He has*
> *created us anew in Christ Jesus, so we can do the good*
> *things he planned for us long ago."*
>
> — Ephesians 2:8-10, NLT

God's grace has us covered; it is our eternal guaranteed insurance. Let me explain in more detail.

Insurance[4] is a means of guaranteeing protection or safety against loss or peril. The extent or breadth of insurance policy coverage is typically offered in different packages or plans. The more extensive the plan, the higher the premium paid; the greater the liability, the higher the cost and vice versa.

When I experience damage or loss of property, I check the insurance policy or contract terms to determine if the item is covered or protected. The policy or contract is my guarantee of compensation for the damage or loss of the item. If the item is not covered, I become troubled and *restlessly* consider other ways to repair or be compensated for the damage; however, if the item is included, I feel relief, ease, and peace; I am at Rest.

In a similar way, God's gift of grace guarantees that the ultimate and highest price He paid for our complete redemption package is secured. God paid the price by giving His *only* Son, Jesus Christ, so that all of us would not perish but have eternal life.[5]

> *"For this is how God loved the world: He gave his one and only Son, so that everyone who believes in him will not perish but have eternal life."*
>
> — John 3:16, NLT

The grace, given by God, secures our complete redemption at the highest cost, showing His limitless generosity and love towards us. This highlights the importance of this divine gift, freely given to those who believe and have faith in Him.

The insurance coverage of grace, offered by God is the ultimate one, as it continuously safeguards our mind, body, and spirit against all known and unknown life issues.

By accepting to live in God's grace, we attain a profound inner **peace** and **healing** that leads to **Rest.**

How do I know that my redemption package includes peace and health? The Bible says Jesus Christ bore all my grief, sorrow, wounds, ill health, and sin, including all matters that try to take away my peace.[6]

> *"Surely He has borne our griefs and carried our sorrows; Yet we esteemed Him stricken, Smitten by God, and afflicted. But He was wounded for our transgressions; He was bruised for our iniquities. The chastisement for our peace was upon Him, and by His stripes we are healed."*
>
> — Isaiah 53:4-5, NKJV

Therefore, just like earthly insurance, we can obtain the benefits of God's redemption contract by believing in its terms, accepting Jesus Christ as our Lord and Saviour, and **Rest**ing in God's grace for coverage. It's that simple.

This is it! God's abundant Grace is the ultimate answer to finding Rest. Welcome to your place of **Rest**.

**"God's abundant Grace is the
ultimate answer to finding Rest."**

Before we begin celebrating this milestone, please take a
moment to think about this question. *Does "Rest in God"
imply that we should refrain from activity or work to earn a
living?* Absolutely not. Working is a source of dignity and
self-respect, while idleness brings poverty, shame, and
dishonour.[7]

In his letter to the Thessalonian church, the apostle Paul
warns against idleness and encourages us to work and earn
our own living.[8] He also advises us to prioritise leading a
peaceful life, focusing on our affairs, and working with our
hands.[9]

So here we have it. I could end this book right here because
we have reached our destination. But I encourage you to
continue reading as I reveal how *retreating*, seeking *refuge*,
and nurturing *relationships* have helped me remain
anchored in God's Rest, drawing inspiration from the story
of Mary and Elizabeth.

Mary and Elizabeth

The first chapter of the book of Luke covers a fascinating
part of the story of our redemption before the birth of Jesus
Christ. Mary, the mother of Jesus, found **Rest** with her rela-
tive, Elizabeth, the mother of John the Baptist.

Beyond their family ties, Mary and Elizabeth bonded over
similar struggles and experiences that affected their physical

(body), mental (mind), and spiritual well-being. I have closely examined these similarities, their relationship, and their significance in finding **Rest**.

- Both Elizabeth and Mary faced societal criticism. Elizabeth was barren,[10] unable to bear children, and carried the weight of this burden into her later years. Meanwhile, Mary, unmarried and pregnant,[11] was at the point of having her engagement broken off and, most likely, expecting that she may be stigmatised.
- The angel, Gabriel, appeared to their partners, Zacharias, the priest (Elizabeth's husband),[12] and Joseph (Mary's betrothed and descendant of David)[13] prior to the births of John the Baptist and Jesus Christ, respectively. Both men initially doubted the messages delivered by the angel Gabriel but, as time passed, they eventually came to accept the truth and blessing.
- Both women carried within them seeds of divine purpose, bringing forth children whose births were prophesied.[14]
- In addition to enduring the physical challenges of pregnancy and childbirth, they also tragically suffered the sorrow, pain, and anguish of losing their sons by government execution.[15]

Identifying these similarities explains why Mary's visit to Elizabeth gave them relief, solace, reassurance, and renewed purpose in their peculiar circumstances. It highlights the importance of seeking refuge and wise counsel. Mary found physical Rest by retreating to Elizabeth's home. Rest for her mind and soul in their relationship, and spiritual Rest in God's grace and promises

Retreat

> *"God rewards humility with grace,*
> *for He gives grace to the humble."*

A retreat[16] is a place of privacy or safety sought for prayer, meditation, study, or instruction. It is also an act or process of withdrawing, especially from what is difficult, dangerous, or disagreeable.

Mary selected Elizabeth's home as a place of retreat, where she stayed for about three months before returning home.[17] Considering the circumstances, it is understandable why she withdrew to a new setting that provided her peace, acceptance, and comfort during her challenging period.

Taking a step back to retreat can bring clarity to the mind, body, and spirit. It provides an opportunity to gain a broader perspective on a situation, enabling clearer thinking and a better chance of achieving one's goals or purpose.

In the preceding chapters, I emphasised the significance of humility and reprioritising our lives. Prioritising God is an act of surrender, obedience, and humility. God rewards humility with grace, for He gives grace to the humble.[18] Retreating from our daily lives to prioritise and honour

God's authority demonstrates our humility and invites His intervention and grace into our lives.

When I encounter complicated life problems that need careful consideration, I have learned to distance myself from the situation and reflect on it. I retreat by withdrawing and submitting myself to my faith in God.

Lately, this has involved being alone in quiet contemplation. I didn't have any specific strategies, religious guidelines, or schedules. I focused on hearing from God by reading my Bible, watching sermons, listening to Christian music, and taking notes.

The importance of choosing positive sights and sounds, highlighted in Chapter Two, inspired me to plan my retreat carefully. I chose a location far from the noise of my daily life, yet still familiar enough to avoid any distractions. Additionally, I ensured the place was secure to guarantee the safety of myself and my belongings.

The serene setting offered nature's quiet and peaceful beauty, allowing me to communicate with God without interruptions. Moreover, it was a place where I was treated with kindness, felt cared for, and fully accepted.

Retreating removed me from the daily routine of deadlines, tasks, and obligations that interrupted my ability to listen to God and give into His Rest. It provided a place to shut off life's cancers, release my heavy burdens to God, and find Rest for my soul.[19]

*"Come to Me, all you who labour and are heavy laden, and
I will give you rest. Take My yoke upon you and learn from
Me, for I am gentle and lowly in heart, and you will find
rest for your souls. For My yoke is easy and My burden is
light."*

— Matthew 11:28-30, NKJV

I found clarity and peace at my retreat. I learnt how to navigate situations that cause turmoil and manage difficult circumstances. Above all else, I treasure the ability to rely on the peace and presence of God, so I protect it.

Safeguarding my inner peace means that I must avoid anything that may disturb it. I know that I must resist negative influences,[20] so I choose, instead, to focus on positive, godly thoughts.[21]

*"...Resist the devil, and he will flee from you. Come close to
God, and God will come close to you."*

— James 4:7b-8, NLT

*"And now, dear brothers and sisters, one final thing. Fix
your thoughts on what is true, and honourable, and right,
and pure, and lovely, and admirable. Think about things
that are excellent and worthy of praise."*

— Philippians 4:8, NLT

Embarking on a personal journey of purpose can be a lonely experience, significantly so when retreating from the comfort and familiarity of our lives; however, with God's guidance, a retreat can help us realise and fulfil our purpose. It provides an opportunity for self-improvement and brings us closer to God's peaceful presence and Rest.[22]

"Prioritise your time with God by retreating."

Seek His face[23] concerning any issues you may have, and everything else will fall into place[24] as you **Rest** in His grace.

> *"But seek first the kingdom of God and His righteousness, and all these things shall be added to you."*
>
> — Matthew 6:33, NKJV

Refuge

Identifying and preparing a place of refuge[25] in advance is essential, especially during difficult times. We all need a safe place that shields us from crisis, danger, or distress. A sanctuary offers empathy and allows us to freely express our fears as it helps to heal our mind, spirit, and body. It is a place to find peace and rest, much like Mary found in the arms and home of Elizabeth.

In August 2017, I received a message that made me realise just how crucial it is to have a place of refuge. This inspired me to create my safe haven, which proved to be a life-saver three years later when I faced a crisis. I'm grateful that I took the time to prepare it because emergencies often come without warning.

My *refuge* is my nest,[26] my *retreat* and my place of **Rest**.

Do you have a place where you feel safe and peaceful? This could be a physical location, person, or something intangible, like a feeling or song. No matter what it is, remember that God's presence brings grace, peace, and Rest, which makes all the difference. I encourage you to establish a place of refuge today.

Relationships

While many people associate a place of refuge with a physical building or location, I have learned that refuge can also be found in *relationships*.

The presence of God is not only found in a specific location but can also be experienced through the people around us. This highlights the significance of cultivating godly relationships with individuals who genuinely care about us. People who have gone through similar trials themselves or are willing to go through our journey with us, sharing in both our pain and triumphs, can be blessings and bring great comfort to us.

Mary and Elizabeth had a unique bond that went beyond their familial ties to each other. Without their friendship, Mary may not have been able to connect with Elizabeth, who was hiding due to her unexpected pregnancy at an older age. As stated in Luke 1:24 (NKJV), Elizabeth hid for five months and expressed gratitude to God for taking away her shame.[27] It is possible that the two women were hiding from their community's judgment; nonetheless, they had a solid and trustworthy relationship that allowed them to access each other in their times of need.

My spiritual refuge is in my relationships. Therefore, it is paramount for me to establish bonds with individuals who provide sound advice, embrace me without judgment, and exude acceptance.

Relationships can set your life's tone and tip the scales favourably between life and death. I know from experience that having positive and encouraging relationships, packed with the power of the Holy Spirit, effectively keeps me hopeful and strong. I am thankful for the relationships that give me refuge.

It's important to be mindful of the messages, reactions, and overall energy we allow into our ears, eyes, and heart, especially during difficult times.[28] Uplifting and optimistic messages, infused with the strength of the Holy Spirit, have a profound life-saving effect.

Some of the messages I received during my time of peril were particularly impactful, and I would like to share them to encourage you.

> "Our God is faithful! He brought you out before, and He'll beat this 'thing' again! Great tests always lead to great testimonies! Your biggest testimony ever is at hand! I am in faith with you, declaring that Christ

took ALL *your sicknesses and bore ALL your
diseases!*

You are HEALED *in Jesus' Name! The Lord is your
strength, health, and the length of your days! You've
got a long, good, and fulfilling life ahead of you! Much
love!*

*Read 2 Corinthians 1:8-10; Psalms 34:15, 18, 19;
Matthew 8:17; 1 Peter 2:24; Isaiah 53:1, 4, 5 (NKJV;
NLT; MSG)."*

—D.S.

August 5, 2020

"Nothing to do, only believe John 6:28-29 (NKJV)...
'What shall we (Darbuni) do, that we (Darbuni) may
work the works (total absolute healing) of God?' Jesus
answered and said to them (Darbuni), 'This is the
work of God, that you (Darbuni) believe in Him
(Jesus) Whom He (God) sent.'[29]

*The greatest miracle in your life happens not by you
working and trying to save yourself but by simply
believing in Jesus, who died to save you from eternal
damnation and give you eternal life. Why, then,
should lesser miracles of healing breakthroughs be
any different?*

*Darbuni, what is that miracle 'you' need today?
There is nothing left for you to do, but everything for*

you to believe because Jesus has already done it all for you."

—N.B.

August 11, 2020

"As the mountains surround Jerusalem (was then and will always be), the Lord God, Jehovah Rapha, surrounds you[30] with His Presence today. Through all you go through, rest in His arms of love. This verse resonated for you—Psalm 125:2 (NJKJV). Morning! God bless."

–P. R.

August 13, 2020

"God is focused on you, Darbuni; without blinking, His eyes are on you. You are covered with joy, blessings, comfort, prosperity, healing, peace, fulfilment, restoration, renewal, and strength. A double life portion of more years in full health, body, mind, and spirit, in the name of Jesus Christ. Amen."

—H. J.

August 16, 2020

"Darbuni, remember these five points:

1. What God has started, He will certainly finish.[31]
2. You are never alone;[32] the presence of the Holy Trinity—God the Father, the Son, and the Holy Spirit

*is always with you without fail. The angels of God are
also with you.*[33]

*3. Talk to God and the Holy Spirit freely. Speak in
tongues often.*[34]

4. Soak yourself in the Word of God and worship[35]
songs—as a way of life.

*5. Set in your mind that you are not sick, for Jesus
Christ took away your sickness long ago.*[36] *You are
only going through the process."*

—H. J.

September 29, 2020

The positive impact of these messages, conveyed to me at a
desperate, despondent, and discouraging time, helped save
my life. I recommend that you cultivate good and genuine
relationships. Additionally, be willing to offer the same
support and spread God's love to others as guided by God.[37]

*"Let us think of ways to motivate one another to acts of love
and good works. And let us not neglect our meeting
together, as some people do, but encourage one another,
especially now that the day of his return is drawing near."*

— Hebrews 10:24-25, NLT

Establishing genuine relationships can be difficult because
only God can truly understand a person's motives and heart.

I have personally experienced my disappointments in this
regard and may have also let others down. No matter the

situation, healthy relationships always provide support and safety.[38]

> "Where there is no counsel, the people fall; But in the multi-tude of counsellors there is safety."
>
> — Proverbs 11:14, NKJV

The Bible guides our relationships,[39] including our connection to habits, places, technology, social media, etc., that may trigger negativity or a lack of peace.

> "Don't be fooled by those who say such things, for "bad company corrupts good character."
>
> — 1 Corinthians 15:33 (NLT)

Taking control of your relationships may require difficult conversations and choices, such as saying no to things that don't align with your values and beliefs. Don't be anxious about this.[40]

> **"People who genuinely care for and love you will accompany you on your path to fulfilling God's purpose."**

Rely on God to guide you towards the right individuals. Once you come across them, you'll experience a natural bond and comfort in your interactions.

"Be anxious for nothing, but in everything by prayer and supplication, with thanksgiving, let your requests be made known to God; and the peace of God, which surpasses all understanding, will guard your hearts and minds through Christ Jesus."

— Philippians 4:6-7, NKJV

To fully experience God's grace and peace, we must give Him complete control over our body, mind, and spirit. By implementing the practice of *Reset, Restoration*, and *Renewal*, we attain perfect harmony and *Rest* in His presence.

Prayer

Dear God,
Thank You for bringing me to my place of Rest.
Thank You for Your love, grace, and peace that never changes.[41] *Help me remember to always retreat into Your presence and seek Your Word. Please help me develop spiritual connections and relationships and teach me to be a place of refuge for others, to the glory of Your Kingdom.* In the name of Jesus Christ, I pray. *Amen.*

Epilogue

T hank you for reading my book.

I would love to say the journey was easy, yielding instantaneous results, but that differs from my story. Though the battle is tough, and the scars are deep and ugly, mine is a story of an accumulation of God's daily miracles. Each day records "small" victories that may seem insignificant but, pulled together, amount to mountains of glorious testimonies that allow me to experience God's love in tangible ways, live my best life, and write this book.

Christians are not granted immunity or shielded from life's storms or afflictions. The devil does not relent, go on vacation, or take seasonal breaks. Life goes on, pulling on our strings as surmounting challenges flow. But what sets us apart is that we serve a God that promises to help, strengthen, hold us up, and deliver us from it all. Glory to God!

"Don't be afraid, for I am with you. Don't be discouraged, for I am your God. I will strengthen you and help you. I will hold you up with my victorious right hand."

— Isaiah 41:10, NLT

Sometimes, I feel overwhelmed and cry to God, asking Him, "How can you let this happen to me? Do you mean I must deal with this too? It's too much for me to bear! Help me, God!"

And just when I release my burdens to Him, coming to the end of myself at the brink of breaking, He sends me help and patiently reassures me, saying, "You are right. It is too much for you to bear, so you should cast *all* your cares on me."[1]

God is faithful to His word.[2] What a loving God we serve.[3] God's love for us sets us apart.

We stand confident in the eye of the storm knowing that, with God, the outcome will always work together for our good.[4]

"And we know that God causes everything to work together for the good of those who love God and are called according to his purpose for them."

— Romans 8:28, NLT

I believe that every person has a void within them that desires to be filled by God, our Heavenly Father and Creator. Often, we try to fill this emptiness by pursuing things like success, status, beauty, wealth, approval, conformity, and even addictive behaviours. We may think that acquiring these things will bring us contentment, but we frequently find ourselves trapped in an endless cycle of pursuing more.

Until we reach the end of ourselves and accept Jesus Christ, we will continue to feel empty, incomplete, and unfulfilled.

Choosing to heed God's voice and walk in His purpose is the most satisfying and rewarding decision I have made in my entire life. The images in this book are my testimony of God's healing grace. May they inspire you to see the possibilities of trusting in God.

God's promise to **Reset**, **Restore**, and **Renew** me brought me into His place of **Rest**.

I hope this book helps you fight and win the battles in life, knowing that God clothes you with the strength to keep going and thrive purposefully.

I pray that you find Rest in God's grace and peace, laced with joyful laughter and hope for a brighter future. Amen.

God bless you.

BIBLIOGRAPHY
HEALING RESOURCES

Online Resources

1. Creflo Dollar, "Biblical Healing Scriptures 3/8/17," YouTube, August 15, 2020, https://youtu.be/DKM6Wvuvato.
2. Dodie Osteen, "Healing Scriptures with Dodie Osteen," YouTube, July 13, 2022, https://youtu.be/1pvdYE6tvoY.
3. Kenneth Copeland Ministries, "What is the Baptism of the Holy Spirit?" YouTube, April 27, 2023, https://www.youtube.com/watch?v=v-UoNoWiwuE.
4. Kenneth E. Hagin, "Baptism of the Holy Spirit," Facebook, April 27, 2023, https://www.facebook.com/MiracleTouchNetwork/videos/kenneth-e-haginbaptism-of-the-holy-spirit/110954834353075/.
5. T. D. Jakes Sermon Series: "Crushing," YouTube, March 19, 2023, https://youtube.com/playlist?list=PLrIOm7ASS08ct5R2zAtmtmcWGarvKcR08.

Book Resources

1. Bosworth, F. F. *Christ the Healer*. Grand Rapids, Michigan: Fleming H. Revell, a division of Baker Book House Company. 1973, 2000.
2. Dollar, Creflo A. Jr. *How to Obtain Healing*. College Park, Georgia: Creflo Dollar Ministries. 1999.

3. Hagin, Kenneth E. *Casting Your Cares Upon the Lord* (Booklet). Tulsa, Oklahoma: Faith Library Publications. 1981.

4. Hagin, Kenneth E. *Faith Food Devotions.* Tulsa, Oklahoma: Faith Library Publications, 2000.

5. Hagin, Kenneth E. *Health Food Devotions* (Paperback). Tulsa, Oklahoma: Faith Library Publications, 2007.

6. Hagin, Kenneth E. *How You Can Be Led by the Spirit of God* (Hardback). Tulsa, Oklahoma: Faith Library Publications. 2006.

7. Hagin, Kenneth E. *Learning to Forget* (Booklet). Tulsa, Oklahoma: Faith Library Publications, 1999.

8. Hagin, Kenneth E. *You Can Have What You Say!* (Booklet). Tulsa, Oklahoma: Faith Library Publications. 1996.

9. Hagin, Kenneth Jr. *Faith Takes Back What the Devil's Stolen* (Booklet). Tulsa, Oklahoma: Faith Library Publications, 1999.

10. Osteen, Dodie. *Healed of Cancer.* Houston, Texas: A Joel Osteen Publication. 1986.

11. Oyedepo, Faith A. *The Power of the Communion Table.* Lagos, Nigeria: Dominion Publishing House. 2011, 2013, 2015.

12. Warren, Rick. *The Purpose Driven Life.* Grand Rapids, Michigan: Zondervan. 2002.

13. Wommack, Andrew. *God Wants You Well.* Tulsa, Oklahoma: Harrison House Publishers. 2010.

NOTES

Introduction

1. "Ubangiji," *Google Translate.* 2023 - Hausa to English, accessed March 22, 2023, *https://translate.google.com/?hl=en&sl=auto&tl=en&text=ubangiji&op=translate.*
2. "Gagara Misali," *Google Translate.* 2023 - Hausa to English, accessed March 22, 2023, *https://translate.google.com/?hl=en&sl=auto&tl=en&text=gagara%20misali&op=translate.*
3. "Ina karfin shaidan in da Yesu yana mulki? Ba bu o sam sam", *Google Translate.* 2023 - Hausa to English, accessed May 12, 2023,: https://translate.google.com/?sl=ha&tl=en&text=Ina%20karfin%20shaidan%20in%20da%20Yesu%20yana%20mulki%3F%20Ba%20bu%20o%20sam%20sam&op=translate.

Preface

1. Merriam-Webster.com Dictionary, s.v. "cancer," accessed May 18, 2023, https://www.merriam-webster.com/dictionary/cancer.

Prologue

1. Merriam-Webster, Incorporated, "revelation," accessed March 13, 2023, https://www.merriam-webster.com/dictionary/revelation.
2. Merriam-Webster.com Dictionary, s.v. "cancer," accessed May 18, 2023, https://www.merriam-webster.com/dictionary/cancer.

1. RESET

1. Acts 9: 1-20 (NLT)
2. Acts 13:9 (NKJV)
3. Merriam-Webster.com Dictionary, s.v. "reset," accessed March 13, 2023, https://www.merriam-webster.com/dictionary/reset.
4. Hebrews 12:5-7 (NLT)
5. Merriam-Webster.com Dictionary, s.v. "cancer," accessed March 13, 2023, https://www.merriam-webster.com/dictionary/cancer.
6. Galatians 1:13-14 (NKJV)
7. John 8:36 (NKJV)
8. Hebrews 8:12 (NKJV)
9. James 4:6-7 (NKJV)
10. Psalm 100:4 (NLT)
11. Psalm 22:3 (KJV)
12. 1 John 1:9 (NKJV)
13. Psalm 51:10-12 (NKJV)
14. 1 John 5:14 (NKJV)

2. RESTORE

1. Acts 9: 1-20 (NLT)
2. Acts 9:8-9 (NLT)
3. Acts 9:11-20 (NLT)
4. Philippians 1:21-22; 4:13 (NKJV)
5. "Emperor Qin's Tomb," *NationalGeographic.com*, Copyright © 1996-2015 National Geographic SocietyCopyright © 2015-2023 National Geographic Partners, LLC. *All rights reserved*, accessed April 10, 2023, https://www.nationalgeographic.com/history/article/emperor-qin.
6. "Men of the People: Restorers bring terracotta army back to life," Copyright © 2020 CGTN. Beijing ICP prepared NO.16065310-3, accessed April 10, 2023, https://news.cgtn.com/news/2021-05-07/Men-of-the-People-Restorers-bring-terracotta-army-back-to-life-104Pck2dkZO/index.html.
7. Matt 10:29-31 (NLT)
8. 1 Corinthians 6:19-20 (NKJV)
9. 1 Timothy 4: 8 (NLT)
10. "How Memory Works," The Derek Bok Center for Teaching and Learning, Copyright © 2023 The President and Fellows of Harvard

College, accessed on May 4, 2023, https://bokcenter.harvard.edu/
how-memory-works.
11. Proverbs 4:23 (NLT)
12. Hebrews 4:12 (NKJV)
13. Philippians 2:9-11 (NKJV)
14. Luke 1:37 (NLT)
15. Acts 1:8 (NLT)
16. 2 Timothy 1:7 (NKJV)
17. 1 Peter 5:10(NLT)
18. James 4:6-7 (NKJV)
19. 1 Peter 5:10 (NLT)
20. Jeremiah 17:14 (NLT)
21. Psalm 51:12 (NLT)
22. Jeremiah 30:17 (NKJV)
23. Luke 11:1-4 (NKJV)
24. Luke 11:9-13 (NKJV)
25. John 14:16-17 (NKJV)
26. Romans 8:16 (NLT)
27. John 16:7 (KJV)
28. John 16:13 (NKJV)
29. Romans 8:10-11 (NKJV)
30. Galatians 5:22-23 (NLT)
31. Acts 1: 1-5 (NLT)
32. Acts 9: 17-18 (NKJV)
33. Acts 2:1-4 (NKJV)
34. Galatians 5:22-23 (NLT)

3. RENEW

1. Luke 5: 36-38 (NKJV)
2. "Wineskin", Wikipedia® is a registered trademark of the Wikimedia
   Foundation, Inc., a non-profit organization, accessed on May 1, 2023,
   https://en.wikipedia.org/wiki/Wineskin.
3. *Why Wineskins? The exploration of a relationship between wine and
   skin containers by Barbara Wills & Amanda Watts*, pdf pages 123 and
   126, accessed May 2, 2023, https://www.academia.edu/33576670/
   Why_Wineskins_The_Exploration_of_a_Relationship_Be
   tween_Wine_and_Skin_Containers.
4. *New Wine, Old Wineskins*, Copyright © 2020 The New Frontier
   Ministries, all rights reserved, accessed May 2, 2023, https://www.

thenewfrontierministries.org/blog/2020/04/07/new-wine-old-wine skins.

5. 2 Corinthians 5:17 (NKJV)

6. Romans 6:1-3 (NLT)

7. Ephesians 4:22-24 (NKJV)

8. Merriam-Webster.com Dictionary, s.v. "vision," accessed May 1, 2023, https://www.merriam-webster.com/dictionary/vision.

9. Merriam-Webster.com Dictionary, s.v. "imagination," accessed May 4, 2023, https://www.merriam-webster.com/dictionary/imagination.

10. Hebrews 11:1 (NLT)

11. Genesis 1 (NKJV)

12. Exodus 25 – 31 (NKJV)

13. Jeremiah 23:5 (NKJV)

14. "Square peg in a round hole," Wikipedia® is a registered trademark of the Wikimedia Foundation, Inc., a non-profit organization, accessed on May 1, 2023, https://en.wikipedia.org/wiki/Square_peg_in_a_round_hole.

15. Merriam-Webster.com Dictionary, s.v. "restructure," accessed May 3, 2023, https://www.merriam-webster.com/dictionary/restructure.

16. Merriam-Webster.com Dictionary, s.v. "reform," accessed May 3, 2023, https://www.merriam-webster.com/dictionary/reform.

17. Psalm 119:160 (NKJV)

18. 2 Corinthians 10:4-5 (NKJV)

19. Ephesians 4:22-24 (NKJV)

20. Romans 12:2 (NLT)

21. "Malaria," accessed June 21, 2023, https://www.who.int/news-room/fact-sheets/detail/malaria.

22. "The Languages of the North Central Geopolitical Zone of Nigeria," accessed June 21, 2023, https://jolan.com.ng/index.php/home/article/download/42/37 .

23. "Malaria," accessed June 21, 2023, https://www.who.int/news-room/fact-sheets/detail/malaria.

24. Merriam-Webster.com Dictionary, s.v. "mosquito net," accessed June 30, 2023, https://www.merriam-webster.com/dictionary/mosquito%20net.

25. "Tsoro," accessed May 12, 2023, https://translate.google.com/?hl=en&sl=auto&tl=en&text=tsoro%0A&op=translate.

26. "Biology: Anopheles Mosquitos," accessed on June 30, 2023, https://www.cdc.gov/malaria/about/biology/index.html#:~:text=The%20biting%20of%20female%20Anopheles%20mosquito,tropical%20regions)%20to%20transmit%20malaria.

27. Isaiah 54:17 (NKJV)
28. Psalm 27: 1-3 (NKJV)
29. Psalm 27: 5 (NLT)
30. Psalm 27:1 (NLT); 1 John 1:5 (NKJV)
31. Psalm 4:8 (NKJV); Matt 11: 28-29 (NKJV)
32. Exodus 14:14 (NKJV)
33. Ephesians 6:11-18 (NLT)
34. 1 John 4:16-18 (NLT)
35. Ephesians 1:7 (NKJV)
36. Psalm 103:4 (NLT)
37. Psalm 34:4–5 (NKJV)

4. REST

1. Merriam-Webster.com Dictionary, s.v. "grace," accessed May 10, 2023, https://www.merriam-webster.com/dictionary/grace.
2. Ephesians 2:8-10, NLT
3. Romans 5:15-18 (NLT); 2 Corinthians 5:21 (NKJV)
4. Merriam-Webster.com Dictionary, s.v. "insurance," accessed May 12, 2023, https://www.merriam-webster.com/dictionary/insurance.
5. John 3:16 (NLT)
6. Isaiah 53:4-5 (NKJV)
7. Proverbs 24:33-34 (NLT); Proverbs 14:23 (NLT)
8. 2 Thessalonians 3: 7-12 (NLT)
9. 1 Thessalonians 4:11-12 (NLT)
10. Luke 1:7 (NKJV)
11. Matthew 1:18-19 (NLT)
12. Luke 1:11-22 (NKJV)
13. Matthew 1:18-25 (NLT)
14. Matthew 1:22-23 (NLT); Isaiah 9:6-7 (NKJV)
15. Matthew 14:10; 27:50 (NKJV) Luke 23:13-25 (NKJV)
16. Merriam-Webster.com Dictionary, s.v. "retreat," accessed April 12, 2023, https://www.merriam-webster.com/dictionary/retreat.
17. Luke 1:56 (NLT)
18. James 4:6 (NKJV); 1 Peter 5:5b (NKJV); Luke 14: 11 (NKJV); Luke 1: 52 (NLT)
19. Matthew 11: 28-30 (NKJV)
20. James 4:7b-8 (NLT)
21. Philippians 4:8 (NLT)
22. John 14:27 (NKJV)

30. Psalms 125:2 (NKJV)31. Philippians 1:6 (NLT)32. Deuteronomy 31:8 (NKJV)

Epilogue

1. 1 Peter 5:7 (NKJV)
2. 1 Corinthians 1:9 (NLT)
3. John 3:16 (NLT)
4. Romans 8:28 (NLT)

Acknowledgments

Writing this book was a battle that became one of my life's most fulfilling and rewarding achievements. I didn't do it alone. Foremost, I give all the glory and thanks to the Almighty God, my Father, who makes everything possible. I thank Him for preserving my life and choosing me to be a vessel in His vineyard.

Unending gratitude to the woman who inspires me to write, an author herself, silent listener, honest sounding board, fierce intercessor, and devoted daughter of the Sovereign God, my mother. She birthed me and continues to nurture and sustain me daily in prayer before the Lord. Thank you, Mom.

Special thanks to my husband and children for being by me through the roughest times and holding me up when I couldn't carry myself. My brothers and sister, for hours and hours of spontaneous intercessory prayer with fasting. To my dear sister, Pemwa, for urging me to write this book and believing it into existence...it is done.

Sharing my story was hard, but she made it easy. Sincere appreciation to Salt Essien-Nelson, a.k.a. "Gishiri," who did not hesitate to embrace this project in its raw state and pour her editorial expertise into it to ensure my story is shared well. Thanks, Gishiri, for mining the treasures in my notes and for your loving spirit, caring heart, and patience.

This book would not be in your hands without the remarkable technical support and invaluable contributions of several people, including the Messenger Unlocking Your Book mentoring team; thank you for making the writing process easy and reminding me of the importance of being an obedient messenger of God. To my great publishing, editing, and marketing team, I couldn't have done this without you. To the incredible TY Bello and her team, your timeless photos captured the essence of a beautiful narrative, then untold; thank you.

I am so grateful to everyone who supported me, offered a kind word, shared a tear, gave a knowing smile, whispered a prayer, sent a warm hug, and posted thoughtful messages. To the voices of God that speak the Gospel of love, life, and hope from the pulpit and through various media, you reached me in my most difficult times; God bless you all.

About the Author

Darbuni is a seasoned chartered public relations practitioner with over twenty years of experience in corporate communications, government relations, brand and reputation management.

From an early age, she learned the values of 'seeking, serving, and following Christ' as a member of the Girls Brigade of Nigeria. This instilled in her a passion for helping others, which led her to actively volunteer and support numerous non-profit organizations and charities. For the past two decades, she has been a partner at the 700 Club-Christian Broadcasting Network (CBN) Africa, a faith-based organization committed to spreading the Gospel, offering hope, and providing essential resources to those in need through community humanitarian relief, children's ministry, and media broadcasting across West Africa.

Darbuni loves spending time with her family and is a devoted mother, daughter, sister, partner, and friend. She also enjoys music, the arts, and travelling, but above all, feels so blessed to be "God's girl."

Made in the USA
Columbia, SC
23 April 2024

34513509R00065